PROPHECIES FULFILLED AND

FULFILLING

Lectures on Prophecy

BY

HENRY CLAY MORRISON

First Fruits Press
Wilmore, Kentucky
c2013

ISBN: 9781621711230 (Print), 9781621711247 (Digital)

Prophecies Fulfilled and Fulfilling: Lectures on Prophecy By Henry Clay
Morrison
First Fruits Press, © 2014
Previously published: Lectures on prophecy by the Pentecostal Publishing
Company, ©1916

Digital version at
http://place.asburyseminary.edu/firstfruitsheritagematerial/75/

For all other uses, contact:

First Fruits Press
B.L. Fisher Library
Asbury Theological Seminary
204 N. Lexington Ave.
Wilmore, KY 40390
http://place.asburyseminary.edu/firstfruits

Morrison, H. C. (Henry Clay), 1857-1942.
    Prophecies fulfilled and fulfilling: lectures on prophecy [electronic
    resource] / by H.C. Morrison.
    1 online resource (101 p) ; digital
    Wilmore, Ky. : First Fruits Press, c2014.
    Reprint. Previously published: Lectures on prophecy. 4th edition.
    Louisville, Ky. : Pentecostal Pub. Co., c1916.
    ISBN: 9781621711247 (electronic)
    1. Bible -- Prophecies. I. Title. II. Lectures on prophecy.
    BS647 .M67 2014eb   236

Cover design by Haley Hill

asburyseminary.edu
800.2ASBURY
204 North Lexington Avenue
Wilmore, Kentucky 40390

First Fruits
THE ACADEMIC OPEN PRESS OF ASBURY SEMINARY

Lectures on Prophecy.

By

H. C. Morrison, D. D.,

Author of "World Tour of Evangelism," "Life Sketches and Sermons," "The Second Coming," "Romanism and Ruin," "The Two Lawyers," "Thoughts For The Thoughtful," "The Confessions of a Back-slider," Etc.

FOURTH EDITION.

PREFACE.

The contents of this book were originally prepared and delivered in the form of lectures, to the students of several colleges. We are sending it forth trusting it may prove suggestive and helpful to all who may read it.

H. C. MORRISON.

DEDICATION.

This volume is lovingly dedicated to all of my friends in the beautiful city of Glasgow, Ky.

CONTENTS.

LECTURE I.

THE WISDOM OF THE PROPHETIC METHOD. THE DEVELOPMENT, THE DISPERSION, AND THE RESTORATION OF THE HEBREWS.

It is impossible to account for creation without admitting the existence of a creator. The universe is so vast, the movement of its numerous planets so harmonious and perfect, the forces that hold the millions of suns in their proper adjustment to each other are so powerful, the evidences of intelligent design are so plainly written everywhere that the thoughtful mind cannot believe that this vast creation is a mere accident. Such an accident is unthinkable. This universe, with its almost innumerable worlds, so harmoniously adjusted to each other and moving in such perfect order, could not exist without a creator.

It is just as impossible to acount for man's existence without a creator as it is impossible to account for the universe without a creator. It is unthinkable

5

that a God so infinitely great as the Creator of this universe should create immortal, moral beings without undertaking to reveal Himself to those beings, and something of their capacity, duty and destiny; something of the laws with which He proposes to govern, adjust and regulate the social relation that should exist for the happiness, welfare, and progress of such beings.

This being true, it is reasonable to expect just such a revelation as we have in the Bible. Intelligent beings would naturally desire a revelation from their Creator bearing indisputable credentials; a revelation capable of positive proof that it is from God; a revelation that can be relied upon without any sort of hesitation or fear that it is an imposition placed upon them by their fellow beings, and without divine origin and authority. The Bible is such a book.

Infinite wisdom could not have chosen a wiser method of revelation than the prophetic method. The prophecies contained in the Old Testament Scriptures, so wonderfully and accurately fulfilled in the unfolding chapters of human history, are positive and infallible proof that the men who wrote the Bible were divinely inspired.

The prophetic method places the Bible beyond the reach of successful contradiction. It would have been impossible for the ancient prophets to have so accurately forecast the coming events of history without inspiration from God. They could not have built the wheel of prophecy so that its cogs would fit so perfectly into the cogs of the onmoving wheel of history had God not revealed to them the coming events of the future.

The prophetic method makes it impossible for the Bible to grow old or obsolete. It is so written that it can never become a book of the past. Fulfilling prophecy, as the years go by, makes the Bible not only a book of today, but a book of tomorrow also. The devout and intelligent student of prophecy may have a good general notion of what the future contains and conduct himself accordingly.

Standing on the mountain peaks of inspired prophecy he looks back along the highway of history, and beholds with delight how accurately prophecy has been fulfilled. Looking into the Bible and then looking on world conditions about him, he beholds the marshalling of the hosts of coming events falling into line and marching forward to the fulfillment of the predictions of the ancient seers of God, and his faith in divine revelation is unshaken and restful.

In studying the Bible it is well to remember that it is largely the history of the Hebrew people. Soon after the account of creation and the flood, we have the calling out of Abraham and the development of a family, the growth of that family into a tribe, the going of that tribe into Egypt, the increasing of that tribe into a multitude. Then Moses appears and leads that multitude out of bondage into the wilderness, Joshua brings them into Canaan, and they become a great nation. Their religious forms, ceremonies and sacrifices, their laws and customs, their priests, judges and kings, their wars, victories and defeats, their backslidings and reclamations, their history, proverbs and psalms, their prophecies concerning their future, the coming Messiah, the nations that surrounded them, and the final redemption of the race and setting up of the kingdom of God in the world make up the Old Testament. It is in this way that God has chosen to reveal Himself, to show to us His attributes, His will, His purposes and methods with men. In the history of the Hebrew people He has revealed to men the blessedness of obedience and holiness and the curse of rebellion and sin.

We wish to call your attention to a few general divisions of the prophecies:

First. Prophecies concerning the development of the Hebrew nation.

Second. Prophecies concerning the dispersion of the Hebrew people among the nations of the earth.

Third. Prophecies relating to the restoration of the Hebrew people to Palestine.

Fourth. Prophecies pointing out the destruction of the nations, cities and peoples who persecuted the Hebrew people.

Fifth. Prophecies concerning the coming and sufferings of Christ.

Sixth. Prophecies concerning the Gospel Dispensation, the second coming, and the glorious reign of Christ.

You will see at once that in five lectures, with so wide a range of prophecy and history, that we shall not be able to treat this great subject with any sort of thoroughness, but shall try to make what we say suggestive. One of the great objects in lecturing to students is not so much to give them thorough and exhaustive information, as it is to arouse within them a desire to seek after information. We are not to undertake to pack your mind with facts, but to try to arouse your mind to a studious search after facts. What we desire to produce in you is mental stimulation—brain hunger—giving you some helpful suggestions that may interest you in, and introduce you to one of the greatest subjects that can possibly claim your attention.

The first scripture to which we call your attention is in Genesis 12:1, 2, 3, verses: "Now the Lord had said unto Abram, get thee out of thy country, and from thy kindred, and from thy father's house, into a land that I will show thee: And I will make of thee a great nation, and I will bless thee and make thy name great; and thou shalt be a blessing: And

I will bless them that bless thee, and curse him that curseth thee; and in thee shall all the families of the earth be blessed."

Notice the promise, "I will make thy name great." No infidel will deny that this promise has been kept. The name of Abraham is known and revered in all the Christian world, and among all Mohammedan peoples. His name has become great. Notice also, "I will bless them that bless thee, and curse him that curseth thee." It is a historic fact that God's judgments have fallen upon the people who have persecuted the Jews.

Notice again: "In thee shall all the families of the earth be blessed." This prophecy also has been, and is being fulfilled. The children of Abraham wrote the Bible, both Old Testament and New. The children of Abraham organized the Church under the Old Dispensation and under the Christian Dispensation. The children of Abraham furnished the prophets and the priests through the long procession of centuries leading up to the coming Messiah, and they furnished the first preachers of the gospel. Moses, Joshua, Joseph,

David, John the Baptist, John the Beloved, and St. Paul were all the children of Abraham. The Christian civilization which has come into the world is a fulfillment of the prophecy that, "In thee shall all the families of the earth be blessed."

We quote again from Genesis, Chap. 17:7 and 8, "And I will establish my covenant between thee and me, and thy seed after thee in their generations for an everlasting covenant, to be a God unto thee and to thy seed after thee. And I will give unto thee, and to thy seed after thee the land wherein thou art a stranger, all the land of Canaan, for an everlasting possession; and I will be their God."

We want you to notice that God's covenant with Abraham and his people is "an everlasting covenant." It is to abide forever. Notice also the land of Palestine is to be "'an everlasting possession." Infidelity, through the past centuries, has been sneering at this promise to the Israelites; they have been robbed of their land with no human appearance of ever having it restored to them; but the sneering infidel

has not understood that the dispersion
of the Hebrew people and the desolation
of their land is also a fulfillment of a
prophecy uttered by Hosea many centuries ago. In the third chapter, 4th
and 5th verses of Hosea's prophecy we
read, "For the children of Israei snall
abide many days without a King, and
without a prince, and without a sacrifice and without an image, and without
an ephod, and without teraphim. Afterward shall the children of Israel return, and seek the Lord their God, and
and David their King; and shall fear
the Lord and His goodness in the latter
days."

We find a very remarkable prophecy
concerning the upbuilding and development of the Hebrew people in Deut.
7:6, 7, and 8 verses. "For thou art a
holy people unto the Lord thy God; the
Lord thy God hath chosen thee to be a
special people unto Himself, above all
people that are upon the face of the
earth. The Lord did not set His love
upon you, nor choose you, because ye
were more in number than any other
people; for ye were the fewest of all
people; But because the Lord loved you,

and because He would keep the oath
which He had sworn unto your fathers,
hath the Lord brought you out with a
mighty hand, and redeemed you out of
the house of bondmen, from the land of
Pharaoh, King of Egypt."

You will see here that God was determined to keep His oath to Abraham.
He is keeping it and will keep it forever. The promises contained in the
Bible to the Israelitish people cannot
fail.

THE DISPERSION OF THE HEBREW PEOPLE.

With reference to the dispersion of
the Hebrew people throughout the nations of the world, it is an interesting
fact that before they had crossed into
Canaan, Moses foresaw their apostasy
and captivity, and gives a startling description of the same in Deut. 28:49-53.
"The Lord shall bring a nation against
thee from far, from the end of the
earth, as swift as the eagle's flight; a
nation whose tongue thou shalt not understand; a nation of fierce counte-
nance, which shall not regard the person of the old, nor show favour to the
young; and he shalt eat the fruit of thy
cattle, and the fruit of thy land, until

thou be destroyed; which also shall not leave thee either corn, wine, or oil, or the increase of thy kine, or flocks of thy sheep, until he have destroyed thee. And he shall besiege thee in all thy gates, until thy high and fenced walls come down, wherein thou trusteth, throughout all thy land; and he shall besiege thee in all thy gates throughout all thy land, which the Lord thy God hath given thee. And thou shalt eat the fruit of thine own body, the flesh of thy sons and of thy daughters, which the Lord thy God hath given thee, in the siege, and in the straitness, wherewith thine enemies shall distress thee."

Moses here describes the siege of Jerusalem and some of the startling events which took place during that siege when the Romans came from afar, bearing on their banners the eagle, the insignia of their swiftness and power; who so utterly destroyed the people and hemmed them in Jerusalem with a siege that drove them frantic with hunger, in which it is a well known fact that parents did eat their own children.

In the same chapter from which we have just quoted, 63rd to 67th verse,

Moses continues to describe even before
the Israelites had crossed into Canaan,
what should afterward befall them,
that which has come to be veritable
history. The prophecy reads as follows:
"And ye shall be plucked from off the
land whither thou goest to possess it.
And the Lord shall scatter thee among
all people, from the one end of the earth
even unto the other; and there thou
shalt serve other gods, which neither
thou nor thy fathers have known, even
wood and stone. And among these nations shalt thou find no ease, neither
shall the sole of thy foot have rest; but
the Lord shall give thee there a tremb-
ling heart, and failing of eyes, and sorrow of mind; and thy life shall hang in
doubt before thee; and thou shalt fear
day and night, and shall have none as-
surance of thy life."

How literally this prophecy has been
fulfilled. The Jews have been persecuted throughout the centuries and in all
parts of the world. They have been
robbed, beaten and slain; they have
lived in uncertainty and dread. Even
within recent years in many European
lands they have been great sufferers,

and today in many countries they are almost without sympathy or protection.

We wish to call your attention to a prophecy contained in Deut. 29:24-28: "Even all nations shall say, Wherefore hath the Lord done thus unto this land? What meaneth the heat of this great anger? Then men shall say, Because they have forsaken the covenant of the Lord God of their fathers, which He made with them when He brought them forth out of the land of Egypt: For they went and served other gods, and worshipped them, gods whom they knew not, and whom He had not given unto them: And the anger of the Lord was kindled against this land, to bring upon it all the curses that are written in this book: And the Lord rooted them out of their land in anger, and in wrath, and in great indignation, and cast them into another land, as it is in this day."

Here the prophet is telling us that it will become the common knowledge and remark of the people as they look upon the desolation of Palestine, the ruined city, and barren and destroyed country that it has been the judgment of God sent upon His people because of their wickedness. This is exactly true at this very time. This is a well known fact among heathen. Mohammedans and travelers, and people everywhere. Long after Moses wrote this prophecy Isaiah said in Chap. 1:7, 8, 9, "Your country is desolate, your cities are burned with fire: your land, strangers devour it in your presence, and it is desolate, as overthrown by strangers. And the daughter of Zion is left as a cottage in a vineyard, as a lodge in a garden of cucumbers, as a besieged city. Except the Lord of hosts had left unto us a very small remnant, we should have been as Sodom, and we should have been like unto Gomorrah." Again Isaiah says, "Upon the land of my people shall come up thorns and briers." The prophet Jeremiah joins in the same sad refrain in Chap. 19:7, 8, 9: "And I will make void the counsel of Judah and Jerusalem in this place; and I will cause them to fall by the sword before their enemies, and by the hands of them that seek their lives; and their carcases will I give to be meat for the fowls of the heaven, and for the beasts of the earth. And I will make this city desolate, and an hissing; every one that passeth thereby shall be astonished and hiss, because of all the plagues thereof. And I will cause them to eat the flesh of their sons, and the flesh of their daughters, and they shall eat every one the flesh of his friend, in the siege and straitness wherewith their enemies, and they that seek their lives, shall straiten them."

Ezekiel looking through the prophetic telescope beheld the same calamities befalling Israel, Chap. 7:1-4: "Moreover, the word of the Lord came unto me, saying: Also, thou son of man, thus saith the Lord God unto the land of Israel, an end, the end is come upon the four corners of the land. Now is the end come upon thee, and I will send mine anger upon thee, and will judge thee according to thy ways, and will recompense upon thee all thine abominations. And my eye shall not spare thee, neither will I have pity, but I will recompense thy ways upon thee, and thine abominations shall be in the midst of thee; and ye shall know that I am the Lord."

The prophet Amos goes on record in harmony with the rest of the inspired seers of Israel, see Chap. 9:9, 10: "'For, lo, I will command, and I will sift the house of Israel among all nations, like as corn is sifted in a sieve, yet shall not the least grain fall upon the earth. All the sinners of my people shall die by the sword, which say, the evil shall not overtake or prevent us." The prophet Micah bears witness to the same destruction of his people. In Chap. 3, verses 10, 11 and 12, he says: "They build up Zion with blood, and Jerusalem with iniquity. The heads thereof judge for reward, and the priests thereof teach for hire, and the prophets thereof divine for money; yet will they lean upon the Lord, and say, Is not the Lord among us? none evil can come upon us. Therefore shall Zion for your sake be plowed as a field, and Jerusalem shall become heaps, and the mountain of the house as the high places of the forest."

You will notice how thoroughly the prophets agree with each other as they describe the calamities which were to befall their people. These prophecies scarcely need comment with reference to their fulfillment. There are no facts more plainly written in history, and more generally understood among all intelligent men in all the world, than those facts in connection with the destruction of Palestine, the fall of Jerusalem, the captivity, scattering, persecutions and sufferings of the Hebrew people. The words of Moses, Isaiah, Ezekiel, Jeremiah, Hosea, Micah and Amos have been literally fulfilled to the smallest detail. The predictions of these men have become plainly written history, and there is no possible way to account for their knowledge of these things centuries before they came to pass, except to agree that the Bible is an inspired book, and that the men who wrote these prophecies which have through succeeding generations and centuries been so accurately fulfilled, were inspired men.

There is a story that during one of his campaigns, the old Emperor William, the grandfather of the present Emperor of Germany, sitting by his camp fire one night said to his chaplain: "Chaplain, what is the best external proof of the inspiration of the Bible? Answer me in a word, not an argument, or discussion; but in a word." The chaplain tipped his cap, and said:

"Sire, the Jews." "Ha!" said the Emperor, "that is splendid! you could not have given a better answer." The Jews as we have them in the Bible, in history, and in the world today are a tremendous external evidence of the inspiration of the Scriptures.

We wish to impress upon your mind the wisdom of the prophetic method of revelation. Could you conceive of any better way, or any other method half so good addressed to intelligent, reasoning beings as this method? This plan of God's to inspire men to write certain predictions of future events in such general account of the conduct of nations, giving such minute details of transactions and incidents that were to occur hundreds and thousands of years after the predictions had been written, and behold as we stand in the midst of history we find that the predictions of the ancient seers of the Lord dovetail into the facts, not only as they have transpired through the years, but the events which are coming to pass in the very times in which we are living.

It seems to us that Christian people could desire no better evidence, or present no stronger proof to the enemies of the Word of God, and unbelievers everywhere, in this skeptical age, of the inspiration of our Bible, than the remarkable accuracy with which prophecy has been fulfilled and is now being fulfilled before our very eyes.

THE RESTORATION OF THE HEBREW PEOPLE.

The prophets just as definitely foretold the restoration of the Hebrew people to Palestine, as they foretold their dispersion and scattering throughout the nations. The fulfillment of the prophecies concerning the dispersion is a positive guarantee that the prophecies concerning the restoration will be literally fulfilled. We can no more reasonably doubt the restoration of the Jews than we can doubt the scattering of the Jews. We wish to call your attention to some of the prophecies concerning the restoration of the Jews. We have already noticed that Moses predicted the captivity and scattering of the Jews before they crossed into Palestine, and we have seen that what

Moses wrote on the subject has been literally fulfilled.

In Deut. 30:1, 2, and 3 verses, he tells us just as plainly that they shall be restored to Palestine: "And it shall come to pass, when all these things are come upon thee, the blessing and the curse, which I have set before thee, and thou shalt call them to mind among all the nations, whither the Lord thy God hath driven thee. And shalt return unto the Lord thy God, and shalt obey His voice according to all that I command thee this day, thou and thy children, with all thine heart, and with all thy soul; That then the Lord thy God will turn thy captivity, and have compassion upon thee, and will return and gather thee from all the nations, whither the Lord thy God hath scattered thee."

In Isaiah we find a graphic description of the gathering of Israel back to Palestine. We will notice the 11th chap. 11th and 12th verses of Isaiah: "And it shall come to pass in that day, that the Lord shall set His hand again the second time to recover the remnant of His people, which shall be left, from Assyria, and from Egypt, and from

Pathros, and from Cush, and from Elam, and from Shinar, and from Hamath, and from the islands of the sea. And He shall set up an ensign for the nations, and shall assemble the outcasts of Israel, and gather together the dispersed of Judah from the four corners of the earth."

We want you to also notice Jer. 23rd Chap. 3rd, 7th and 8th verses: "And I will gather the remnant of my flock out of all countries whither I have driven them, and will bring them again to their folds; and they shall be fruitful and increase. Therefore, behold, the days come, saith the Lord, that they shall no more say, The Lord liveth, which brought up the children of Israel, out of the land of Egypt: But, the Lord liveth, which brought up and which led the seed of the house of Israel out of the north country, and from all countries, whither I had driven them; and they shall dwell in their own land."

Take also the quotation from the 31st Chap. 10th, 11th and 12th verses: "Hear the word of the Lord, O ye nations, and declare it in the isles afar off, and say, He that scattered Israel will gather him, and keep him, as a shepherd doth his flock. For the Lord hath redeemed Jacob, and ransomed him from the hand of him that was stronger than he. Therefore, they shall come and sing in the height of Zion, and shall flow together to the goodness of the Lord, for wheat, and for wine, and for oil, and for the young of the flock, and of the herd: and their soul shall be as a watered garden; and they shall not sorrow any more at all."

Also note the 33rd chapter of Jer. 7th and 8th verses: "And I will cause the captivity of Judah and the captivity of Israel to return, and will build them, as at the first. And I will cleanse them, from all their iniquity, whereby they have sinned against me; and I will pardon all their iniquities, whereby they have sinned, and whereby they have transgressed against me."

We are taught in the Scriptures that there is not only to be a great gathering of this dispersed people from all countries back to Palestine, but there is also to be among them a great spiritual awakening. This fact is brought out very clearly in a beautiful prophecy found in Ezekiel 36th Chap., 22nd to 31st verses: "Therefore say unto the house of Israel, Thus saith the Lord God: I do not this for your sakes, O house of Israel, but for mine holy name's sake, which ye have profaned among the heathen, whither ye went. And I will sanctify my great name, which was profaned among the heathen, which ye have profaned in the midst of them; and the heathen shall know that I am the Lord, saith the Lord God, when I shall be sanctified in you before their eyes. For I will take you from among the heathen, and gather you out of all countries, and will bring you into your own land. Then will I sprinkle clean water upon you, and ye shall be clean: from all your filthiness, and from all your idols, will I cleanse you. A new heart also will I give you, and a new spirit will I put within you; and I will take away the stony heart out of your flesh, and I will give you an heart of flesh. And I will put my spirit within you, and cause you to walk in my statutes, and ye shall keep my judgments, and do them. And ye shall dwell

in the land that I gave to your fathers;
and ye shall be my people, and I will be
your God. I will also save you from all
your uncleannesses: and I will call for
the corn, and will increase it, and lay
no famine upon you. And I will multi-
ply the fruit of the tree, and the increase of the field, that ye shall receive
no more reproach of famine among the
heathen. Then shall ye remember your
own evil ways, and your doings that
were not good, and shall loathe your-
selves in your own sight for your iniquities and for your abominations."

We wish in conclusion to call your attention to the fact that devout Bible
students throughout the world are quite
agreed that we are now on the eve of
the fulfillment of those prophecies concerning the restoration of the Jews. In
fact, they have in the last few years
been returning to Palestine in large
numbers. Jerusalem for two decades,
has been rapidly rebuilding. Large
numbers of houses have been going up
outside the city walls. A few years ago
we spent some days in the city of Jerusalem, and were profoundly impress-
ed with the rapid growth of the city,

and the large number of Jews returning from various countries.

It is quite remarkable, and ought to be a source of great joy to Christian people, that just at this time when destructive criticism is so aggressive, the prophetical portions of the Scriptures are being so literally fulfilled. In His Infinite wisdom God anticipated and has provided for every emergency that can possibly arise, and ever has His answers ready for the enemies of truth and righteousness. We praise His great name that the book He has given us upon which we have founded our hopes of peace and happiness here, and eternal blessedness yonder, is so written that it is capable of positive proof that it is divinely inspired.

LECTURE II.

PROPHECIES CONCERNING THE DESTRUC-
TION OF THE CITIES AND NA-
TIONS WHO PERSECUTED
THE JEWS.

We propose in this lecture to call attention to a few of the prophecies pointing to the calamities that were to fall upon the peoples who persecuted the Jews. We wish to impress upon your mind the fact that these prophecies were uttered at a time so remote from their fulfillment, when the cities and nations against which they were uttered were so powerful and prosperous that, from a human point of view, they would abide until the end of time; yet these prophecies were fulfilled so perfectly, with such minute details that it lifts the whole matter entirely out of the realm of guesswork or any possibility of mere human foresight, into the realm of divine inspiration.

In a word, the men whose prophecies

are contained in our Bible and who foretold the coming, sufferings, death, and glorious reign of our Lord Jesus Christ, were inspired men. Their predictions about other matters of God's dealings with the nations of the earth have so perfectly fitted into the facts of history, that there is no reasonable ground for doubting the truth of their claims, and no way to account for the accurate matter in which they foretold future events except to admit that they were inspired and that God spoke through them.

We wish to call your attention to the City of Nineveh. It was the capital of the Assyrian Empire and one of the most ancient cities of the world, evidently beginning its existence not a long while after the flood.

In Genesis, 10th chapter and 11th verse, we are told that Asshur went forth and built Nineveh. When Jonah was called to preach to the Ninevites we are told that it was "an exceeding great city of three days' journey." Twenty miles in those times was a day's journey, so it was sixty miles around the city of Nineveh. The wall encircling the city was one hundred feet high and so broad that three chariots could drive around it abreast. On this wall there were fifteen hundred towers about two hundred feet high. If an enemy had have been able to climb upon the city wall, the defenders could have gone into these towers and showered down missiles and stones upon them.

When Jonah was displeased because God did not destroy the city at the time of his preaching and God was making a plea for mercy, He said to Jonah that there were more than six-score thousand people in the city who could not discern between their right hand and their left. That is, there were more than one hundred and twenty thousand babies in the city who were not old enough to know their right hand from their left hand. The general estimate of populations is one baby to every five persons. So Nineveh must have had at that time a population of more than six hundred thousand people. It was the Metropolis of one of the most wealthy and powerful Empires in the world, and was one of the most bitter haters and persecutors of the Jewish people. Such was Nineveh when the prophet of God foretold its overthrow, utter ruin and desolation.

If you will read the books of Kings and Chronicles you will find that the Kings of Assyria were the unrelenting enemies of the Jews.

Pul, a King of Assyria, invaded Israel and was bought off with a thousand talents of silver. (2 Kings 15:19). Later on "Shalmaneser, the King of Assyria, came up throughout all the lands;" and after a long siege "took Samaria and carried Israel away into Assyria," and scattered them about in various cities. (2 Kings 17:5, 6). Still later, Sennacherib, King of Assyria, came up against all the fenced cities of Judah and took them (2 Kings 18:10-13) and he exacted of good King Hezekiah "three hundred talents of silver, and thirty talents of gold," and Hezekiah had to empty his own treasuries in the palace and the treasuries of the Lord's House in order to meet this immense levy and induce the King to leave the country. Still later on Esarhaddon, King of Assyria, Son of Sennacherib, finally completed the destruction of Israel, taking the people away

captive into Assyria, and bringing people from Cuthah, Hamath, and Babylon
and placing them in the cities of Israel
which had been left empty and desolate
by the captivity and removal of their
inhabitants to Assyria.

There is an account of the result of
this transplanting of the heathen people
into Palestine given in 2 Kings, 24-30
verses. We read here that these trans-
planted heathen became so wicked that
God sent wild beasts to destroy them,
and when word was brought to the
King of Assyria he sent back a Hebrew
priest to teach them the ways of God,
but this priest was not a successful
missionary and the people continued to
worship their idols.

Now let us examine some of the prophecies pronounced against these de-
spoilers of Israel and Nineveh, their
great capital city. In Zephaniah 2nd
chapter, 13th to 15th verses, we read of
the judgments of God to be sent upon
Nineveh. And He will stretch out His
hand against the north, and destroy Assyria; and will make Nineveh a desolation, and dry like a wilderness."

"And flocks shall lie down in the

midst of her, all the beasts of the nations: both the cormorant and the bittern shall lodge in the upper lintels of it: their voice shall sing in the windows; desolation shall be in the threshholds: for He shall uncover the cedar work."

"This is the rejoicing city that dwelt carelessly; that said in her heart, I am, and there is none beside me: how is she become a desolation, a place for beasts to lie down in every one that passeth by her shall hiss, and wag his hand."

This prophecy has been so literally fulfilled that it takes experienced, well versed and discerning travelers to locate the place where this great city once stood. The scattered ruins indicate the large area once covered by the city, but now the place is perfectly desolate, a broken and rugged pasture where the cattle browse and lie down to rest.

The Prophet Nahum gives a graphic description of the coming destruction of Nineveh while it was yet in its glory in chapter 1, verses 1, 2, and 3; also 8, 9, 10, and 14 verses we read the following:

"The burden of Nineveh. The book of the vision of Nahum the Elkoshite."

"God is jealous, and the Lord revengeth; the Lord revengeth, and is furious; the Lord will take vengeance on His adversaries, and He reserveth wrath for His enemies."

"The Lord is slow to anger, and great in power, and will not at all acquit the wicked: the Lord hath His way in the whirlwind and in the storm, and the clouds are the dust of His feet."

"But with an overrunning flood He will make an utter end of the palace thereof, and darkness shall pursue His enemies."

What do you imagine against the Lord? He will make an utter end: affliction shall not rise up the second time. For while they be folden together as thorns, and while they are drunken as drunkards, they shall be devoured as stubble fully dry."

"And the Lord hath given a commandment concerning thee, that no more of thy name be sown: out of the house of thy gods will I cut off the graven image and the molten image; I will make thy grave; for thou art vile."

Herodotus tells us that the Medes assisted the Babylonians in capturing the

city of Nineveh. The city was besieged
for a long while, but with its powerful
walls the inhabitants felt perfectly safe.
During the siege there was a long heavy
rain which caused the river which
flowed through the city to overflow its
banks and break down a part of the city
wall. Note the prophecy of Nahum:
"With an overrunning flood He will
make an utter end of the place thereof.
Diodorus Siculus, the historian, tells us
that the soldiers of the Assyrian army
were drunk when the city was captured
and that when the King saw that the
overflowing river had broken the walls
and the defences of the city, he gathered
his people into the palace and setting it
on fire, was consumed.

Note the prophecy again: "For while
they be folden together as thorns, and
while they are drunken as drunkards,
they shall be devoured as stubble fully
dry." It will be seen here that the
prophet not only told of the destruction
of the city but described the details of
its destruction. How men with these
facts before them, with the cogwheels
of prophecy fitting so perfectly into the
cogwheels of history, can doubt the in-

spiration of the prophets, we are unable
to comprehend.

We should remember, however, that
the average unbeliever has not taken
time or pains to study with thoughtful
care the prophecies contained in the Old
Testament Scriptures and the perfec-
tion with which these prophecies have
been fulfilled. It seems to us that our
religious teachers have not used, as they
might, these great facts to give to Christians a broad and unshakable foundation upon which to rest their faith in the
inspiration of the Holy Scriptures, and
to prove to doubters the unquestioned
fact of the divine inspiration of the men
who wrote the prophecies.

BABYLON.

We wish to call attention briefly to
some prophecies concerning the fall of
Babylon, the capital of the Babylonian
Kingdom. Babylon was as ancient, as
great and as wicked a city as Nineveh,
and was equally the bitter enemy and
persecutor of the Jewish people. While
the King of Nineveh had deported the
ten tribes of Israel and carried them
into captivity, the King of Babylon had

conquered Judah, destroyed Jerusalem and carried the two remaining tribes of the Hebrew people into captivity. Jeremiah, in his grief over the ruin of his people, says, "Israel is a scattered sheep; the lions have driven him away; first, the King of Assyria hath devoured him, and last this Nebuchadnezzar, king of Babylon, hath broken his bones."

"Therefore thus saith the Lord of hosts, the God of Israel; Behold, I will punish the King of Babylon and his land, as I have punished the king of Assyria."

We wish to impress upon your minds the fact that the prophecies I shall quote concerning the overthrow of Babylon, were uttered while the city was at the zenith of its power and glory, seemingly invincible to every foe, and with every promise of abiding while time shall last. Yet the prophet of God not only predicted its overthrow and the circumstances connected with its utter ruin, but he names the conqueror of Babylon more than a hundred years before that great military genius was born. The only way to account for such accurate penetration into the future is explained

in Isaiah 46:9, 10:   "I am God, and
there is none like me. Declaring the
end from the beginning, and from ancient times the things not yet done."

Isaiah's prophecies concerning the
fall and ruin of Babylon were written
about one hundred and fifty years before the events described in those prophecies took place. In the 13th chapter
of his writing, 19-22 verses, we find this
remarkable statement:

"And Babylon, the glory of kingdoms,
the beauty of the Chaldees' excellency,
shall be as when God overthrew Sodom
and Gomorrah."

"It shall never be inhabited, neither
shall it be dwelt in from generation to
generation; neither shall the Arabian
pitch tent there; neither shall the shepherds make their fold there:"

"But wild beasts of the deserts shall
lie there: and their houses shall be full
of doleful creatures: and owls shall
dwell there, and satyrs shall dance
there."

"And the wild beasts of the islands
shall cry in their desolate houses, and
dragons in their pleasant palaces: and

her time is near to come, and her days shall not be prolonged."

There are many prophecies in Isaiah concerning the overthrow of this wicked city. It is in the 45th chapter that he mentioned Cyrus as the destroyer of Babylon:

"Thus saith the Lord to His anointed, to Cyrus, whose right hand I have holden, to subdue nations before him; and I will loose the loins of kings, to open before him the two leaved gates; and the gates shall not be shut."

"I will go before thee, and make the crooked places straight: I will break in pieces the gates of brass, and cut in sunder the bars of iron."

"And I will give thee the treasures of darkness, and hidden riches of secret places, that thou mayest know that I, the Lord, which shall call thee by thy name, am the God of Israel."

"For Jacob my servant's sake, and Israel mine elect, I have even called thee by thy name; I have surnamed thee, though thou hast not known me."

"I am the Lord, and there is none else, there is no God beside me: I girded thee, though thou hast not known me:"

The Prophet Jeremiah has much to say against Babylon. In chapter 51, verses 61-64 we read:

"And Jeremiah said to Seraiah, When thou comest to Babylon, and shalt see, and shalt read all these words; Then shalt thou say, O Lord, thou hast spoken against this place, to cut it off, that none shall remain in it, neither man nor beast, but that it shall be desolate forever."

"And it shall be, when thou hast made an end of reading this book, that thou shalt bind a stone to it, and cast it into the midst of Euphrates:"

"And thou shalt say, Thus shall Babylon sink, and shall not rise from the evil that I will bring upon her: and they shall be weary. Thus far are the words of Jeremiah."

Jeremiah names the dates when the city was to be captured. We find this prediction in chapter 25, verses 12-13: "And it shall come to pass, when seventy years are accomplished, that I will punish the king of Babylon, and that nation, saith the Lord, for their iniquity, and the land of the Chaldeans, and will make it perpetual desolations."

"And I will bring upon that land all my words which I have pronounced against it, even all that is written in this book, which Jeremiah hath prophesied against all the nations."

He also gives the details of the capture. "I have laid a snare for thee, and thou art also taken, O Babylon, and thou wast not aware; thou art found, and also caught, because thou hast striven against the Lord." Jer. 50:24.

Babylon is suddenly fallen and destroyed. Jeremiah 51:8; also 30, 31, 32 verses: "The mighty men of Babylon have forborne to fight, they have remained in their holds: their might hath failed; they became as women: they have burned her dwelling places; her bars are broken."

"One post shall run to meet another, and one messenger to meet another, to shew the king of Babylon that his city is taken at one end. And that the passages are stopped, and the reeds they have burned with fire, and the men of war are affrighted."

Cyrus captured Babylon by turning the river which ran through the city out of its course, and at the same time two

armies entered the city, one beneath the
wall where the river entered the city,
and the other where the river left the
city so that the watchman who ran from
the either side of the city to notify the
king that an enemy had entered Babylon, fulfilled the prediction that one post
or messenger should meet another carrying the message to the king of the
fall of the city.

The Prophet Daniel tells us of the
fall of Babylon. It was during a night
of revelry and drunkenness. "They
brought the golden vessels that were
taken out of the temple of the house of
God which was at Jerusalem; and the
king, and his princes, his wives, and his
concubines, drank in them. They drank
wine, and praised the gods of gold, and
of silver, or brass, of iron, of wood and
of stone. In the same hour came forth
the fingers of a man's hand and wrote
over against the candlestick upon the
plaister of the wall of the king's palace:
and the king saw the part of the hand
that wrote."

You remember that Daniel was called
to interpret the writing, and translat-
ed it to the king. "Thou art weighed

in the balances, and art found wanting."

While this was transpiring the invading army was entering the city and that night the king was slain, his army and city destroyed.

It was foretold that Babylon "Shall become heaps." It is a well known fact that the site of this ancient city is a vast succession of mounds, rubbish and ruins.

The prophet said the "wild beasts of the desert" were to "lie there" and "their houses to be full of doleful creatures." In the ruins of Babylon the cellars and pits and holes have become the dens and hiding places of lions and various wild beasts.

The prophet said that Babylon would become "pools of water." Arabs and others seeking after treasure and historical data have dug many holes and pits in the old sight of Babylon, and the Euphrates overflowing has filled these excavations and they have become permanent pools of water.

The desolation of Nineveh and Babylon were seen and accurately described by God's inspired prophets in minute detail many decades before these proph-

ecies were fulfilled, and the sights of
these ancient ruined cities stand today
exactly as foretold by the men of God,
solemn witnesses of the inspiration of
the Holy Scriptures.

If time permitted we might call attention to prophecies concerning the destruction of Tyre, Egypt, and Syria, and
their literal fulfillment in every detail
of the prophetic predictions.

We wish to impress upon you that
there are prophecies written by these
same prophets which have not yet been
fulfilled, but it seems to us that what
of their foretelling which has come to
pass with such accuracy offers a firm
foundation for our belief in their inspiration and that we may, without doubt,
look forward to the fulfillment of what
they have written concerning time yet
to come.

If God punished the nations which
sinned against Him in the past, He will
undoubtedly punish the nations which
have sinned against Him in these latter
times.

It seems that the next fearful fulfillment of prophecy will fall upon the
Turkish nation. No people have been

more bitter in their hatred of the Lord's people, both Jews and Christians, than have the Turks, and no people in all history have been more merciless than they. Throughout the centuries they have slaughtered, robbed, burned, wasted and oppressed the Lord's people.

The Turks have had possession of Palestine and all the countries surrounding that country, for about one thousand two hundred and sixty-nine years. It has seemed strange that the Christian nations have permitted them to hold on to the Holy Land, and trample down Jerusalem as long as they have.

The explanation of it is that God fixes dates and men cannot change them. No power could destroy Nineveh or Babylon until God's time arrived, and then no power could save them. Their destruction was sudden and awful. The prophets have plainly predicted the overthrow of the Turks, but in the mind of God there is a time fixed for that event to take place and neither diplomats or soldiers can hurry or retard Him.

"Jerusalem shall be trodden down of

the Gentiles, until the times of the Gentiles be fulfilled." Luke 21:24. The
word Gentile meant in Bible times what
the word heathen means today. Jerusalem was to be trodden down of the
heathen Turks for an appointed time.

There are two great events spoken of
by the prophets, the fulfillment of which
is now at the door. One is the overthrow
of the Turkish power; the other is the
return of the Jews. These events will
evidently occur almost simultaneously;
the Turks going out just before the
Jews come in. In fact, these prophecies are now being fulfilled before our
eyes; the power of Turkey is being brok-
en and the Jews are beginning to return.

You need not be surprised if some
fearful tragedies take place in a very
short time. The Turks will most likely
make a last desperate stand, but God
will punish them for all their bloody
brutality to His people. He will collect
off of them both the interest and the
principal. Turn to your Bible and read
in Ezk. 35th chapter: "Moreover, the
word of the Lord come unto me, saying,
Son of man, set thy face against Mount

Seir, and prophesy against it, And say
unto it, Thus saith the Lord God, Behold, O Mount Seir, I am against thee,
and I will stretch out mine hand against
thee, and I will make thee most desolate.   I will lay thy cities waste, and
thou shalt be desolate; and thou shalt
know that I am the Lord."

"Because thou hast had a perpetual
hatred, and hast shed the blood of the
children of Israel by the force of the
sword in the time of their calamity, in
the time that their iniquity had an
end:"

"Therefore, as I live, saith the Lord
God, I will prepare thee unto blood, and
blood shall pursue thee; sith thou hast
not hated blood, even blood shall pursue thee."

Read also the 13th and 14th verses
of the same chapter: "Thus with your
mouth ye have boasted against me, and
have multiplied your words against me:
I have heard them.   Thus saith the
Lord God, When the whole earth re-
joiceth, I will make thee desolate."

Isaiah in his visions saw the same destruction coming upon the Turks and
the peoples who with them have op-

pressed the Lord's people. Read in the
34th chapter of his prophecy: "Come
near, ye nations, to hear; and hearken,
ye people; let the earth hear, and all
that is therein: the world, and all things
that come forth of it."

"For the indignation of the Lord is
upon all nations, and His fury upon all
their armies: He hath utterly destroyed
them, He hath delivered them to the
slaughter."

"Their slain also shall be cast out, and
their stink shall come up out of their
carcases, and the mountains shall be
melted with their blood."

"And all the host of heaven shall be
dissolved, and the heavens shall be roll-
ed together as a scroll: and all their
host shall fall down, as the leaf falleth
off from the vine, and as a falling fig
from the fig tree."

"For my sword shall be bathed in
heaven: behold, it shall come down upon
Idumea, and upon the people of my
curse, to judgment."

"The sword of the Lord is filled with
blood; it is made fat with fatness, and
with the blood of lambs and goats, with
the fat of the kidneys of rams: for the

Lord hath a sacrifice in Bozrah, and a great slaughter in the land of Idumea."

There seems to be here some hint of the punishment of the nations in the present war. We have no doubt that by the time this awful war comes to an end the power of Turkey will be broken. Through the centuries the Turks, both in diplomacy and on the battle-field, have been well-nigh invincible, but their time is up. The Italians whipped them, the Balkans whipped them, the Russians are chasing them, and the British will drive them out of Egypt. In a short time they will be compelled to leave Palestine, and, in the not distant future, the Jews who will have fulfilled the time of their dispersion, will come flocking home to the Holy Land like doves to their windows.

LECTURE III.

PROPHECIES CONCERNING THE COMING AND SUFFERINGS OF CHRIST.

According to our chronology it was approximately 4,156 years from the fall of Adam in the Garden of Eden to the death of Jesus Christ on the cross of Calvary. But from the time of that fatal fall to the time of that tragic crucifixion there was strung all along the highway of human history a telegraphic line of prophecy bringing to sinful men the promise of a Redeemer. The first hint of hope to fallen man is given in the promise that. "the seed of the woman shall bruise the serpent's head." From Mt. Moriah Abraham saw the day of Christ, and was glad.

We think there are three facts that will be readily admitted by all students of the Scriptures.

First, the ancient Hebrew prophets saw in their visions, and promised in their messages a coming Redeemer and

King. The harmony of their predictions with reference to this coming Redeemer is most remarkable. The casual
reader will soon discover that the different prophets living in various countries and at periods of time wide apart,
spoke of the same Christ. There are no
contradictions or disagreements among
the prophets concerning the world's
Messiah. Their combined drawings
make up a complete picture of the
Christ. Their combined writings con-
tain His earthly history long before He
was born.

Second, Jesus Christ claimed to be
the promised Messiah. He claimed to
be the one of whom the prophets had
spoken through the years. He never
hesitated to identify Himself as the sent
of God in fulfillment of the prophecies
and promises of the ancient seers of
Israel. He held to this claim when
He knew it meant crucifixion and He
testified to the same after His resurrection.

Third, the writers of the Gospels and
Epistles contained in the New Testament, believed without question in the
inspiration of the prophets, and the di-

vine truthfulness of what they had
written. They also believed, without
doubt, that Jesus of Nazareth was the
Messiah spoken of by the prophets, and
that His personality, life, teaching,
death and resurrection fulfilled what
these ancient prophets had written of
Him.

There is no more interesting or
profitable study than to take the Old
Testament statements concerning the
coming life and sufferings of Jesus, and
the New Testament containing the account of the earthly life, ministry and
sufferings of Jesus, and note how perfectly the Christ life fits into the prediction of the prophets. There is no
way to account for this except that
we agree that the prophets were inspired and Christ was divine.

It must be understood that much prophecy contained in the Old Testament
does not have direct reference to Christ
in that wonderful book. We find prophecies concerning the growth, pros-
perity, and fall of Israel, the dispersion
of the Jews, and their final restoration.
We also find many predictions concerning the fate that was to overtake the

various nations, cities, and peoples who persecuted the Jews. It must be borne in mind that in some places the prophets are speaking of Christ in connection with His first coming into the world, and in other prophecies they are describing the glory of His second coming. The devout student of the word of God will delight to search the Scriptures and classify these various prophecies, note the fulfillment of those pertaining to His first coming and look forward with hopeful joy to the fulfillment of those prophecies that refer to His second coming.

There was one conversation which took place between the Lord Jesus and two of His disciples, which we can but wish might have been recorded in the New Testament. It was that conversation on the road to Emmaus directly after the resurrection. You remember He was walking with two of His disciples who did not recognize Him. They were lamenting over the death of their Lord and were quite puzzled with regard to some rumor they had heard with reference to His resurrection. Believing Jesus to be a stranger in the community they undertook to give Him some outline of the events which had just taken place. Jesus noting their failure to comprehend the great truth of revelation, said to them: "O fools, and slow of heart to believe all that the prophets have spoken; And beginning at Moses and all the prophets, He expounded unto them in all the scriptures the things concerning Himself."

What a wonderful opening up and application of prophecy this must have been. We can but wish some inspired pen might have caught the words and put them down as they fell from His lips. We suppose He quoted to them the words of Moses—"A prophet shall the Lord, your God, raise up unto you from among your brethren, like unto me; Him shall you hear." Perhaps He mentioned the lifting up of the brazen serpent in the wilderness for the healing of the smitten people. He may have quoted Job's saying—"I know that my Redeemer liveth."

If, in the conversation, the disciples referred to the cruelness with which Jesus was crucified, He could have appropriately quoted to them Psalm 22:7 and

8 verses, "All they that see me laugh me to scorn; they shoot out the lip, they shake the head, saying, He trusted on the Lord that He would deliver Him: let Him deliver Him, seeing He delighted in Him." You recall this language was uttered in derision of our Lord while He was hanging on the cross. He could have also called their attention to the 18th verse of the same psalm, "They part my garments among them, and cast lots upon my vesture."

He perhaps reminded them of Zechariah 11:12th and 13th verses, "And I said unto them, if ye think good, give me my price; and if not, forbear. So they weighed for my price thirty pieces of silver. And the Lord said unto me, cast it unto the potter; a goodly price that I was priced at of them. And I took the thirty pieces of silver, and cast them to the potter in the house of the Lord." He must have quoted them Micah 5:2, "But thou Bethlehem Ephratah, though thou be little among the thousands of Judah, yet out of thee shall He come forth unto me that is to be ruler in Israel; whose goings forth have been from of old, from everlasting."

He could hardly have omitted calling
their attention to the 53rd Chapter of
Isaiah, 3rd to 12th verse, which so viv-
idly describes the humble person, and
the patient sufferings of the Lord Jesus! "He is despised and rejected of
men; a man of sorrows, and acquainted
with grief: and we hid as it were our
faces from Him; He was despised, and
we esteemed Him not. Surely He hath
borne our griefs, and carried our sorrows: yet we did esteem Him stricken,
smitten of God, and afflicted. But He
was wounded for our transgressions,
He was bruised for our iniquities: the
chastisement of our peace was upon
Him; and with His stripes we are heal-
ed. All we like sheep have gone astray;
we have turned every one to his own
way; and the Lord hath laid on Him the
iniquity of us all. He was oppressed,
and He was afflicted, yet He opened not
His mouth: He is brought as a lamb to
the slaughter, and as a sheep before
her shearers is dumb, so He openeth not
His mouth. He was taken from prison
and from judgment: and who shall declare His generation? for He was cut off
out of the land of the living: for the

transgression of my people was He stricken. And He made His grave with the wicked, and with the rich in His death; because He had done no violence, neither was any deceit in His mouth. Yet it pleased the Lord to bruise Him; He hath put Him to grief: when thou shalt make His soul an offering for sin, He shall see His seed, He shall prolong His days, and the pleasure of the Lord shall prosper in His hand. He shall see the travail of His soul, and shall be satisfied: by His knowledge shall my righteous servant justify many; for He shall bear their iniquities."

This prophecy of Isaiah concerning our Lord, is one of the most remarkable in all the Old Testament Scriptures. Isaiah described the humble person of Jesus, tells of His patient sufferings, how that He was led as a lamb to the slaughter, and is dumb as a sheep before the shearers. The prophet looking into the centuries ahead beholds the stripes laid upon our Lord, sees Him numbered with the malefactors, and finally buried in a rich man's tomb. Those of you who are acquainted with the circumstances of the crucifixion of Christ know how perfectly these ancient prophecies were fulfilled in all their details. Isaiah standing many centuries in advance of these events, describes them as if he had been an eye witness. There is no possible way to account for this except that Isaiah was divinely inspired, as he claimed to be.

We wish to call your attention to another prophecy of Isaiah, contained in the 7th Chapter, 14th verse: "Therefore the Lord Himself shall give you a sign: Behold, a virgin shall conceive and bear a son, and shall call His name Immanuel." You know this remarkable scripture was fulfilled. In the 16th Psalm and 10th verse, we read this prophecy: "For thou wilt not leave my soul in the grave, neither wilt thou suffer thy holy one to see corruption." The Psalmist is telling us beforehand of the resurrection, and that the body of Jesus would not decay in the tomb.

In the 22nd Psalm, and 21st verse, David gives us the very words that Jesus repeated on the cross hundreds of years afterward. "My God, My God, why hast thou forsaken me." In the 24th Psalm, 7th and 8th verses, we have a beautiful prophecy, representing the return of Christ to the throne of glory after His resurrection: "Lift up your heads, O ye gates; and be ye lift up ye everlasting doors; and the King of glory shall come in. Who is this King of glory? The Lord strong and mighty, the Lord mighty in battle." In Zech. 9th Chap., 9th verse, we have a prophecy which was fulfilled in the most remarkable manner: "Rejoice greatly, O daughter of Zion; shout, O daughter of Jerusalem: behold, thy King cometh unto thee: He is just, and having salvation; lowly, and riding upon an ass, and upon a colt, the foal of an ass."

You well remember that when Jesus approached Jerusalem He sent His disciples, instructing them that they would find a colt tied on which man had never ridden. They were to bring the colt to Him, which they did, and He rode upon the colt into the city of Jerusalem while the people met Him and followed Him, shouting out their words of praise, fulfilling the ancient prophets' prediction in every detail.

In Exod. 12th Chap., 46th verse, in giving the law concerning sacrifice, the

Hebrews were instructed that no bone of the passover lamb should be broken. In John 19th Chap., he gives us the following account, beginning with the 32nd verse: "Then came the soldiers, and brake the legs of the first, and of the other which was crucified with Him. But when they came to Jesus, and saw that He was dead already, they brake not His legs; But one of the soldiers with a spear pierced His side, and forthwith came there out blood and water. And he that saw it bare record and his record is true: and he knoweth that he saith true, that he might believe. For these things were done, that the scripture should be fulfilled, A bone of Him shall not be broken."

In Psalm 22, 16th verse, we have David saying: "They pierced my hands and my feet." In John 19:37, we have him saying, "And again another scripture saith, they shall look upon Him whom they pierced." Long before the crucifixion of our Lord the prophet had described a transaction which took place at the foot of the cross on the day of the crucifixion. It is mentioned in Psalm 22:18, "They part my garments among them, and cast lots upon my vesture." In Jno 19:23, 24, we read, "Then the soldiers, when they crucified Jesus, took His garments, and made four parts, to every soldier a part; and also His coat; now the coat was without seam, woven from the top throughout. They said, therefore among themselves, let us not rend it, but cast lots for it, whose it shall be that the scripture might be fulfilled, which saith, they parted my raiment among them, and for my vesture they did cast lots. These things therefore the soldiers did."

Now we should like to impress upon your minds the fact that long before Jesus was born it was prophesied that He should be the son of a virgin, and so He was. You remember the incident: Joseph had decided to put away Mary after he had married her, but was restrained from doing so by revelation from God. It was prophesied that Jesus should be born in Bethlehem of Judea, and when the Wise Men came to Jerusalem seeking Him they secured the written prophecy, looked into them and found that Jesus was to be born in Bethlehem. They then went forward and found Him there. You will recall that one of the prophets speaking of the Messiah, says, "Out of Egypt have I called my son;" and you will recall that after the death of Herod God did call Joseph and Mary with Jesus up out of the land of Egypt, and they came up out of Egypt.

The prophet said the Messiah would be sold for thirty pieces of silver. Jesus Christ was betrayed by one of His disciples for thirty pieces of silver. The prophet had written long ago that the price paid for Jesus would go to buy land in the potters' field for a burial place. You remember that Judas cast the thirty pieces of silver in the temple and the Hebrew priest gathered up the same, and used the money to purchase the potters' field.

The prophet said the Messiah would make His grave with the rich in His death. Our Lord Jesus was buried in the sepulchre of a rich man.

LET US RECAPITULATE.

The Messiah was to be born of a virgin.

He was to be born in Bethlehem of Judea.

He was to come out of Egypt.

He was to ride into Jerusalem on an ass' colt.

He was to be betrayed by His supposed friend.

He was to be sold for thirty pieces of silver.

The price paid for Him was to be given for the potters' field.

He was to be crucified among thieves.

His enemies were to cast lots for His vesture.

Not a bone of Him was to be broken.

They were to look upon Him whom they had pierced.

He was to be buried in the tomb of a rich man.

All these things were prophesied long before Jesus Christ was born into the world. Every reader of the New Testament is aware that all of these predictions were literally fulfilled in all their details.

There is no possible way to account for these prophecies and their fulfillment, unless we agree that the prophets who wrote them were inspired, and that Christ who fulfilled them is the Son of God. This same inspired book in Old Testament and New, teaches us that all those who truly repent of their sins and trust in the Lord Jesus Christ shall be saved; that in His suffering and death upon the cross, and triumphant resurrection there is salvation full and free for all men from all sin. To His great name be glory and praise forever. The Bible is the word of God. Jesus Christ is the Son of God. He lived, He died, He arose again, and is at this very hour at the right hand of the Father making intercession for the sins of the people. He will come back again in great glory to reign and rule over those who trust in Him for salvation.

LECTURE IV.

PROPHECIES CONCERNING THE GOSPEL DISPENSATION AND THE SECOND COMING OF CHRIST.

In studying the prophecies concerning the Messiah, contained in their sacred writings, the Jews living on the earth during the period of our Lord's ministry among men, failed to get anything approaching a proper conception of Christ's person and mission in the world. To the ordinary reader of the Scriptures, it seems quite remarkable that the Jews should have so misunderstood, hated, and persecuted the Lord Jesus. To us it seems that His personality, teachings, and life fitted so perfectly into the prophecies concerning Him that anyone at all acquainted with those prophecies would have identified Him at once as the Messiah.

Why did the Jews fail to understand and recognize Jesus as the Messiah? First of all, they were in a fearful state of spiritual apostasy and blindness. Spiritual things are spiritually discerned and they were without this divine illumination so necessary to understand the things of God.

Second, they did not understand that it was the plan of God that Christ in accomplishing the task assigned Him, was to come twice into the world. No one in ancient or modern times can rightly divide, properly understand, or correctly interpret the Scriptures who does not recognize this fact. If we desire to get anything approaching a correct and satisfactory comprehension of the true meaning of prophecy, concerning Jesus Christ, we must divide those prophecies into at least two general groups. These groups might be subdivided into several other groups.

There is a group of prophecies which foretells Christ's coming, suffering and death, with the inauguration of the Gospel Dispensation. There is another group of prophecies that tells of Christ's coming in power, to set up His kingdom and reign over His redeemed people, clearly indicating the glory and power of that kingdom and reign. The Jews failed to understand this great fact, and as a consequence they could not rightly divide and properly group the prophecies concerning the Messiah. They lost sight of all those prophecies that referred to the humiliation and sufferings of Christ, and fixed their minds only upon those prophecies which pointed to the restoration of Israel, the overthrow of their enemies, and the glorious rule and reign of their Messiah.

In their thinking and planning they cut out the gospel, or Church age, entirely, and put the kingdom age in its place. They had so misread the prediction and promises of the prophets that they were not looking for a Redeemer from sin to set up a kingdom of righteousness, peace and joy in the hearts of men. In their spiritual blindness they had no conception or desire for a Savior from sin. They did not desire spiritual salvation. They wanted political salvation. They were not looking for an evangelist preaching righteousness, but for a king breaking the yoke of Rome. There were the Scriptures before them. Isaiah had declared in chapter 32:1, 2, "Behold, a King shall reign in righteous-

ness, and princes shall rule in judgment.
And a man shall be as a hiding place
from the wind, and as a covert from
the tempest; as rivers of water in a dry
place; as a shadow of a great rock in a
weary land."

Jeremiah had said in chapter 23,
verses 4 and 5, and part of 6th verse:
"And I will set up shepherds over them,
which shall feed them, and they shall
fear no more, nor be dismayed, neither
shall they be lacking, saith the Lord.
Behold, the day is come saith the Lord,
that I will raise up unto David a righteous Branch, and a King shall reign and
prosper and shall execute judgment and
justice in the earth.   In his days Judah
shall be saved and Israel shall dwell
safely."

Daniel in explaining Nebuchadnezzar's dream, had said, "And in the days
of these kings shall the God of heaven
set up a kingdom, which shall never be
destroyed; and the kingdom shall not be
left to other people, but it shall break
in pieces and consume all these kingdoms and it shall stand forever."   It
never occurred to the Jews for a mo-
ment that while all these scriptures

were absolutely true, and had reference
to the humble Nazarene standing in
their midst, that the fulfillment of these
prophecies belonged to a future age in
the history of the world, an entirely
different dispensation of the grace of
God—a time far removed from the time
in which they were living. The Jews
were blinded with sin, prejudices and
ambition. No people in any age, in
such a state of mind, can discern correctly the simplest truths of God.

When the meek and lowly Christ ap-
peared among them, claiming to be the
long promised Messiah, they could see
nothing in Him that met their conception of their coming King. They were
disgusted and angered with His claims,
and with the rebukes He administered
to them. They were startled as they
saw the influence He had over the masses of the people and determined to put
Him to death for fear that His follow-
ers would inaugurate a revolt against
the authority of Rome, which they were
quite sure would lead to severe vengeance and a more tyrannical adminis-
tration of Roman rule. They hated Jesus on general principles, and determin-

ed to take His life as a sort of political necessity. In their blindness they had no real conception of what they were doing. While suffering on the cross, Jesus looked down on the jeering mob and prayed, "Father, forgive them; they know not what they do."

These Jews could not possibly understand Christ, or properly interpret the prophecies concerning Him, because they did not understand that in the great scheme of human salvation and restoration of divine order in the world it was the plan of God that Christ was to come twice into the world. The first time He was to make His advent through the open door of the stable; the second time He was to make His advent from the open heaven. The first time He was to come in great humiliation; the second time He was to come in great glory. The first time He was to ride into Jerusalem on an ass's colt; the second time He was to ride into Jerusalem on a cloud of glory. The first time He was to hang upon the cross and die amidst the derision of the multitude; the second time He was to sit upon the throne of the universal empire and reign in glory over His redeemed peoples.

All of these facts were plainly written in the prophetical Scriptures, but the Jewish people had so misread prophecy that they got their program at least two thousand years ahead of the divine plan. A large portion of the Christian Church under the New Dispensation has so failed to understand the prophecies that she has gotten her program two thousand years behind the divine plan. The Jews wanted to put the Messiah on the throne, when in the divine order He was due on the cross. They wanted to be crowning a king, when they should have been worshiping the Babe of Bethlehem. A large per cent. of the Christian Church want to linger about Bethlehem, worshiping the Babe cradled in the manger, when they ought to be trimming their lamps and putting on their white robes to meet their coming King. The Jews ignored Christ as a Savior, and clamored for the restoration of Israel. The Christians largely overlook the prophecies concerning our coming King, and desired to build up a great ecclesiasticism.

History repeats itself. The Jews

failed because they did not understand
that Christ must needs come twice into
the World.   For this reason they were
not able to divide the prophecies concerning Him, placing one group about
the humiliation and sufferings of His
first coming, and the other group about
the power and glory of His second coming.   The Christian Church has largely
failed in her great mission in the world
for the same reason.

The program of Christ was to come
into the world, meek and lowly, to live
before men, and teach them the way of
salvation, to die for them, and to set
on foot an aggressive evangelism, which
is to make haste in carrying the gospel
through all the world to every creature.
While this evangelism was going forward He was to go and prepare a place
for His people.   When the gospel had
been preached through all the world for
a witness, He was to return in the
clouds and catch away His bride, the
true Church, and then the wicked multitudes who have rejected the gospel in
the spirit of lawlessness and anarchy
will bring upon themselves "The Great
Tribulation."   Then Christ will return

with His Church and cast Satan out of the world and reign over the earth in peace and righteousness for a thousand years. After that thousand years of reigning, Satan will be loosed for a little season, and then the end will come, bringing in the final judgment.

Almost two thousand years have passed since Christ commissioned His disciples to go into all the world and preach the gospel to every creature, and yet there are hundreds of millions of people within sixty days' travel of this spot, who have never heard of Jesus Christ. Why has the Church failed to accomplish the work assigned her by our Lord? Because she has set up a program of her own entirely out of harmony with the divine plan. She has said, "Our Lord delayeth His coming." Let us rule the earth. She has substituted evangelism with ecclesiasticism. The men who ought to have gone carrying the gospel to neglected millions, have sought office and power in the ecclesiasticism. The money that should have been used to spread the gospel among the lost multitudes, has been expended to support Popes, Cardinals,

Bishops, Secretaries, and a great host of officials, both in the Roman Catholic and the Protestant Churches. Church dignitaries have lived in pomp and luxury while the heathen have gone unevangelized. Meanwhile this army of ecclesiastical officials has drawn the minds of the people away from the saving gospel, the coming of Christ, and His kingdom in the world, and the importance of careful preparation for that great event, and have filled their minds with sectarian prejudice, denominational strife and bitterness.

The money that should have built a chapel on every hill and in every valley in all heathen lands, has gone into vast temples, gorgeous cathedrals, and magnificent churches. Millions of dollars have been used to pile up great towers, and lofty domes, not built out of a pure love of the Christ, or any thought of the world's evangelization or the Lord's return, but built out of a spirit of sectarian pride, and ecclesiastical strife, and ambition to eclipse other ecclesiastical organizations.

Had the Church properly interpreted prophecy, had she understood that

Christ in harmony with the divine program, was coming twice into the world, the first to suffer, die, and set on foot the Gospel Dispensation, to send out an earnest evangelism, to sweep speedily over the earth, offering repentance and salvation to the race—of course, establishing the Church with the pastorate in the wake of this ever advancing evangelistic movement, until the human race should hear the gospel, and then that Christ should come again in glory and power to cast out Satan, overthrow wickedness, and reign and rule in righteousness. We say, had the Church properly interpreted prophecy, how different her history would be written.

With what zeal the early disciples who saw and understood the great truth of our Lord's return, spread the gospel! How rapidly, without railroads, steamships, automobiles, or any of the modern methods of rapid transit they carried the gospel to the various nations and people of their time, and this too, without an organized Church, with rich treasuries to meet their expenses, without any Boards or Secretaries to direct and conserve their work; all they had

was a command and promise from their
Lord and Master. The command was,
"Go ye into all the world and preach the
gospel," and the promise was, "Lo, I
am with you alway, even unto the end
of the world."

How quickly the Church of today,
with her millions of members, and hundreds of millions of money, methods of
travel, wireless telegraphy, the printing
press, and close touch with the ends of
the earth, with open doors to every nation, could carry the gospel to every
creature, if she could only grasp the
great truth that the mission of Jesus
Christ in the world was not to set up
ecclesiasticisms, to debate and war with
each other in their strife and bitterness,
losing sight of the great doctrines of
regeneration, sanctification, the spread
of the gospel to all nations, and the
coming of the Lord.

There are no prophecies in the Old
Testament that indicate that Christ
would be crowned King of a universal
empire at His first coming into the
world. There are no prophecies in the
Old Testament indicating that the Gospel Dispensation will bring in a day of

universal peace and righteousness on the earth.

There is not a hint in the teachings of Christ, or His inspired apostles, that during the Gospel Dispensation the entire population of the world will be brought to repentance, saving faith, and into harmony with God and peace and fellowship among all men.

Inspired teaching is the exact reverse of this. Jesus Christ said to His disciples, "Behold, I send you forth as sheep among wolves." He promised them nothing in this world but crosses, reproach, self-sacrifice and suffering. In the midst of all this they were to have spiritual victory. He said to them, "In the world ye shall have tribulation, but be of good cheer, I have overcome the world." In the parable of the tares and the wheat, we are taught that this dispensation is to be one of mixed good and evil, and will be so until the harvest time, the end of the dispensation when the separation shall take place. Jesus teaches that at His coming to catch away His bride many will be unprepared to receive Him. This truth is brought out with great force in the parable of the wise and foolish virgins.

If the preaching of the gospel is to
bring in the millennium of perfect social
conditions, the purity of men, and the
glory of God upon the earth, and at the
end of this golden age Jesus is to come,
how is it that this parable of the wise
and foolish virgins so clearly teaches
that when He does come a large per
cent. of those who have some knowledge
of Him and some belief in Him will be
unprepared to meet Him.   If the postmillennial teaching is true, the parables
of the wheat and the tares and the wise
and foolish virgins, are incapable of intelligent interpretation.   The postmillennial teaching of the Lord's coming no
more harmonizes with the teachings of
the New Testament than the Jewish
notion of the Messiah appearing as
King of kings and Lord of lords at His
first coming into the world, harmonizes
with the Old Testament teaching.

Let us with humility and reverence
inquire of the Lord about this matter.
"Gracious Master, will the preaching of
the gospel have such a blessed effect upon the world that everybody on the
earth will be saved and ready to meet
thee at thy coming?"   Find His ans-

wer in Matthew 24:7th and 14th verses: "For nation shall rise against nation, and kingdom against kingdom; and there shall be famines, and pestilences, and earthquakes, in divers places. All these are the beginning of sorrows. Then shall they deliver you up to be afflicted, and shall kill you; and ye shall be hated of all nations for my name's sake. And then shall many be offended, and shall betray one another, and shall hate one another. And many false prophets shall arise, and shall deceive many. And because iniquity shall abound, the love of many shall wax cold. But he that shall endure unto the end, the same shall be saved. And this gospel of the kingdom shall be preached in the world for a witness unto all nations: and then shall the end come."

"But Lord, some people think there will be a thousand years of perfect peace and happiness on the earth, just before thy coming. Please tell us about this."

"Immediately after the tribulation of those days shall the sun be darkened, and the moon shall not give her light, and the stars shall fall from heaven, and the powers of the heavens shall be

shaken: And then shall appear the
sign of the Son of man in heaven: and
then shall all the tribes of the earth
mourn, and they shall see the Son of
man coming in the clouds of heaven
with great power and great glory. And
He shall seend His angels with a great
sound of a trumpet, and they shall gather together His elect from the four
winds, from one end of heaven to the
other.   Now learn a parable of the fig
tree; when his branch is yet tender,
and putteth forth leaves, ye know that
summer is nigh: So likewise ye, when
ye shall see all these things, know that
it is near, even at the doors."

"But, Lord, will not the preachers so
understand and explain thy Word to
the people that they will all comprehend
the divine plan and be saved, and be expecting thee and ready to receive thee
with joy at thy coming?"

The Lord's answer to this question
proves the postmillennial doctrine utterly unscriptural.   He says:

"For as in the days that were before
the flood they were eating and drink-
ing, marrying and giving in marriage,
until the day that Noe entered into the

ark, and knew not, until the flood came, and took them all away; so shall also the coming of the Son of man be. Then shall two be in the field; the one shall be taken, and the other left. Two women shall be grinding at the mill; the one shall be taken, and the other left. Watch therefore; for ye know not what hour your Lord doth come."

What are we to think of men who, in the light of these words of Jesus Christ, will persist in telling us that our Lord delays His coming, for ten, fifty, a hundred thousand, or perhaps a million years; and that the ecclesiastical forces of this world will bring all men into a state of perfect peace and righteousness before the Lord comes? Meanwhile an apostate church is tearing up the Bible, denying the deity of Christ, defending and excusing sin, and ridiculing the idea of Christian Holiness.

At the present time almost every white soldier in the European war has been baptized in the name of the Lord Jesus. The British are members of the Episcopal Church, the Germans are members of the Lutheran and Catholic churches, the Russians belong to the

Greek Church, the Austrians, French and Belgians are Roman Catholics. The inhabitants of the Belgian State are largely members of the Roman and Greek churches. These great masses of church members, fighting and killing each other, with their religious teachers and leaders, know little more of the real Gospel, the plan of God, the mission of Christ to save men and His second coming to reign over them, than did the Jewish people who lived on the earth at the time of Christ's ministry among men.

Our only hope for the world is the coming of our Lord to set up His kingdom and rule among men; then, and not until then, will there be universal peace and happiness. Ask the Apostle Paul if he believes the entire human family will be saved before the coming of Christ, and he will answer you in 1st Thess. 5:3-6: "For when they shall say, peace and safety; then sudden destruction cometh upon them, as travail upon a woman with child; and they shall not escape. But ye, brethren, are not in darkness, that that day should overtake you as a thief. Ye are all the children of light, and the children of the day. We are not of the light, nor of darkness. Therefore, let us not sleep, as do others; but let us watch and be sober."

This admonition of the apostle, "Let us not sleep, as do others," shows that when our Lord comes He will find some who are spiritually asleep in unpreparedness. He tells us that sudden destruction will come upon them. Sudden destruction could not come upon anybody at the coming of the Lord if the postmillennial theory was correct, and everybody had been saved for a thousand years before the coming of the Lord.

The whole tenor and teaching of the Scriptures plainly reveal the fact that when Jesus Christ shall appear in His glory multitudes of people will be unprepared to receive Him. Paul in his letter to Timothy reminds him that the "Spirit speaketh expressly, that in the latter times some shall depart from the faith, giving heed to seducing spirits, and doctrines of devils; speaking lies in hypocrisy, and having their conscience seared with a hot iron."

Note also 2nd Timothy, 3d chapter,

first to third verses: "This know
also, that in the last days per-
ilous times shall come. For men
shall be lovers of their own selves,
covetous, boasters, proud, blasphemers,
disobedient to parents, unthankful, un-
holy. Without natural affection, truce-
breakers, false accusers, incontinent,
fierce, despisers of those that are good,
traitors, heady, highminded, lovers of
pleasure, more than lovers of God; having a form of godliness, but denying the
power thereof: from such turn away."

These words of Paul to Timothy make
it very clear that he was not postmillennial in his views. He tells us that
these will be the conditions existing in
the world when Christ appears; and
this teaching of Paul harmonizes perfectly with the teachings of Christ.

Let us put the Apostle Peter on the
witness stand and see what he has to
say on this subject. You will find that
he does not expect the present Gospel
Dispensation to bring everybody into a
state of full salvation. In his second
epistle, chapter 3, he says: "Knowing
this first, that there shall come in the
last days scoffers, walking after their

own lusts, and saying, Where is the promise of His coming? for since the fathers fell asleep, all things continue as they were from the beginning of the creation. For this they willingly are ignorant of, that by the word of God the heavens were of old, and the earth standing out of the water and in the water. Whereby the world that then was, being overflowed with water, perished."

The 10th verse of this same chapter is very suggestive, and shows us that the second coming of Christ will be at a time when the people are not expecting Him. Peter says: "But the day of the Lord will come as a thief in the night." The 14th verse exhorts us with the following impressive language: "Wherefore, beloved, seeing that you look for such things, be diligent that ye may be found of Him in peace, without spot and blameless." In the 17th verse of this same chapter, we are warned against the possibility of "Being led away with the error of the wicked, and falling from our stedfastness."

So it is clearly revealed that up to the end of this age of gospel opportunity, Satan will be in the world, temptation and sin on every hand and we are to watch and pray while we await the coming of the Bridegroom. Throughout the gospel age men may accept or reject the Lord Jesus, and many will reject the gospel as they always have done. The millennium age will begin when John's vision is fulfilled, which is described in Revelation 20th, 1st to 6th verses: "And I saw an angel come down from heaven, having the key of the bottomless pit and a great chain in his hand. And he laid hold on the dragon, that old serpent, which is the Devil, and Satan, and bound him a thousand years. And cast him into the bottomless pit, and shut him up, and set a seal upon him, that he should deceive the nations no more, till the thousand years should be fulfilled: and after that he must be loosed a little season. And I saw thrones, and they sat upon them and judgment was given unto them: and I saw the souls of them that were beheaded for the witness of Jesus, and for the word of God, and which had not worshipped the beast, neither his image, neither had received his mark upon their foreheads, or in their hands; and they lived and reigned with Christ a thousand years. But the rest of the dead lived not again until the thousand years were finished. This is the first resurrection. Blessed and holy is he that hath part in the first resurrection: on such the second death hath no power, but they shall be priests of God and of Christ, and shall reign with Him a thousand years."

Then shall be fulfilled all those splendid prophecies concerning the glory of the Messiah's kingdom and reign, which the Jews in their misunderstanding of the prophecy expected to be fulfilled when Jesus came into the world to introduce the Gospel Dispensation, and die upon the cross for lost humanity. Those Christians who have misread prophecy and believe that the preaching of the gospel will bring in the millennium are just as certainly doomed to disappointment as were those Jews who expected Jesus to restore Israel and set up His kingdom in the world two thousand years ago.

When Christ comes the second time, then a nation will be born in a day; then shall that petition in our Lord's prayer be answered, "Thy kingdom come, Thy will be done on earth as the angels do it in heaven." Then will the kingdoms of this world become the kingdoms of our Lord Jesus Christ. Then shall the knowledge of the glory of the Lord cover the earth as the waters cover the sea.

The wheels of time are turning rapidly. Events in history are crowding in rapid succession upon each other. The prophecies that must be fulfilled before the coming of our Lord are almost complete. The entire thinking world is expecting some great event, some tremendous crisis. There are four great prophecies that will be fulfilled just before the appearing of our Lord Jesus in His glory.

First, the gospel of the kingdom must be preached to all nations.

Second, there must come a great apostasy in the Church.

Third, the Jews must return to Jerusalem.

Fourth, there must come great tribulation on the earth.

All of these prophecies are now being rapidly fulfilled before our eyes, and evidently in the not distant future the predictions contained in this book, Old Testament and New, from Prophets, Christ and the Apostles, shall have been fulfilled, and our Lord shall appear in His glory. May He grant us grace to be prepared to met Him with joy.

LECTURE V.

THE GLORIOUS REIGN OF CHRIST.

The Book of Revelation is a prophetical book abounding in figures and striking imagery. It is an unveiling of those tremendous tragedies in human history that are to take place as we approach the end of the Gospel Dispensation.

In the beginning of this book we have this language, which seems to have been largely overlooked by most Bible readers: "Blessed is he that readeth, and they that hear the words of this prophecy, and keep those things which are written therein: for the time is at hand." Rev. 1:3.

There is fixed in the minds of men a great and comforting faith that some time in the history of the human race, between this and the great Judgment Day, there is coming upon this earth a great triumph of peace over war, of right over wrong, of plenty over want, of happiness over sorrow, when error shall be dethroned and truth shall reign in righteousness

Philosophers have dreamed of this time and longed for the tranquillity and peace it will bring. Statesmen have seen it from afar and called it "The Golden Age." Poets have sung of it in the moments of their highest inspiration. All of these torches of human hopefulness that have illuminated the rugged pathway of the fallen race, were lighted from the fires that burned in the hearts of the ancient prophets who, in the ages gone, promised that the kingdoms of this world shall become the kingdoms of our Lord Jesus Christ; that the time will come when the implements of war will be beaten into implements of husbandry, and the knowledge of the glory of the Lord will cover the earth as the waters cover the sea. Christians call this age of Christ's triumph and reign the Millennium.

In the 20th chapter of the book of Revelation we have a most graphic description of the inauguration of this glorious age. Those persons who are unfriendly to the thought of Christ's reign on earth for a thousand years, have said that this passage in Revelation is the only Scripture of its kind to be found in the Bible. It is quite evident that such persons have not had eyes to see the plainly written word of God.

The angels who stood by the disciples when Jesus ascended into heaven said to them, "In like manner shall He return again." In 1 Thess. 4:15 and 18, we have from the pen of the Apostle Paul a most graphic description of the return of our Lord. "For this we say unto you by the Word of the Lord, that we which are alive and remain unto the coming of the Lord shall not prevent them which are asleep. For the Lord Himself shall descend from heaven with a shout, with the voice of the archangel, and with the trump of God, and the dead in Christ shall rise first: Then we which are alive and remain shall be caught up together with them in the clouds, to meet the Lord in the air: and so shall we ever be with the Lord. Wherefore comfort one another with these words."

Zechariah 14:4, is in perfect harmony with Paul in Thessalonians and the 20th chapter of Revelation. He says: "And His feet shall stand in that day upon the Mount of Olives, which is before Jerusalem on the east, and the Mount of Olives shall cleave in the midst thereof toward the east and toward the west, and there shall be a very great valley: And half of the mountain shall remove toward the north, and half of it toward the south."

Daniel 7:27, is in perfect agreement with Zechariah, Paul and Revelation. "And the kingdom and dominion, and the greatness of the kingdom under the whole heaven, shall be given to the people of the saints of the most High, whose kingdom is an everlasting kingdom, and all dominions shall serve and obey Him."

In the light of these Scriptures, the 20th chapter of Revelation does not appear so lonely as by some had been supposed.

But, you say, if Christ is to reign on the earth a thousand years, it would seem that there would be some reference in the Bible to the condition of things that will exist during that thousand years; something of what will occupy man during that glorious period. We are glad that the Holy Scriptures are not silent on this subject. Zechariah gives us a most interesting passage with reference to that glorious period. Let us read the 14th chapter, verses 8 to 11, and 16 to 20. "And it shall be in that day, that living waters shall go out from Jerusalem; half of them toward the former sea, and half of them toward the hinder sea: in summer and in winter shall it be. And the Lord shall be king over all the earth: in that day shall there be one Lord, and His name one. All the land shall be turned as a plain from Geba to Rimmon south of Jerusalem: and it shall be lifted up, and inhabited in her place, from Benjamin's gate unto the place of the first gate, unto the corner gate, and from the tower of Hananeel unto the king's wine presses. And men shall dwell in it, and there shall be no more utter destruction: but Jerusalem shall be safely inhabited."

"And it shall come to pass, that every one that is felt of all the nations which came against Jerusalem shall even go up from year to year to worship the King, the Lord of hosts, and to keep the feast of tabernacles. And it shall be, that whoso will not come up of all the families of the earth unto Jerusalem to worship the King, the Lord of hosts, even upon them shall be no rain. And if the family of Egypt go not up, and come not, that have no rain; there shall be the plague, wherewith the Lord will smite the heathen that come not up to keep the feast of tabernacles. This shall be the punishment of Egypt, and the punishment of all nations that come not up to keep the feast of tabernacles."

"In that day shall there be upon the bells of the horses, *holiness unto the Lord;* and the pots in the Lord's house shall be like the bowls before the altar."

There are many other impressive and beautiful passages of scripture describing this wonderful reign of our blessed Redeemer, but we shall only call your attention to one more, found in Isaiah 65th chapter, from 19th to the 25th verse. "And I will rejoice in Jerusalem, and joy in my people: and the voice of weeping shall be no more heard in her, nor the voice of crying. There shall be no more thence an infant of days, nor an old man that hath not filled his days: for the child shall die an hundred years old; but the sinner being an hundred years old shall be accursed. And they shall build houses, and inhabit them; and they shall plant vineyards, and eat the fruits of them. They shall not build, and another inhabit; they shall not plant, and another eat: for as the days of a tree are the days of my people, and mine elect shall long enjoy the work of their hands. They shall not labour in vain, nor bring forth for trouble; for they are the seed of the blessed of the Lord, and their offspring with them. And it shall come to pass that before they call, I will answer; and while they are yet speaking, I will hear. The wolf and the lamb shall feed together, and the lion shall eat straw like the bullock: and dust shall be the serpent's meat. They shall not hurt nor destroy in all my holy mountain, saith the Lord."

Some devout people have been unable to get the second coming of Christ divorced in their mind from the thought

of the general judgment. It will be
seen that in the 20th chapter of Revelation the second coming of our Lord and
the general judgment are separated by
a thousand years and a little season.
After the thousand years of the reign
of Christ, Satan is to be loosed. These
prophecies which we have just read are
a description of conditions that will exist during the thousand years of Christ's
reign. It is not describing a heavenly
state but an earthly state—conditions
that will exist in this world after Satan
is bound and Jesus Christ is reigning in
righteousness.

Then all of those splendid Scriptures
that the Jews were so eager and so ex-
pectant of seeing fulfilled when Christ
was on earth at His first coming, will
be gloriously realized. You remember
that the disciples themselves were deep-
ly interested in the reign of Jesus and
were expecting to see Him set up His
kingdom. It was with this expectation
in mind that James and John went to
Jesus, asking for the right and left hand
seats in His glory during His triumphant reign in Jerusalem. It was with
this thought in mind, after the resur-

rection that the disciples said, "Lord, wilt thou at this time restore again the kingdom of Israel?"

Revelation teaches that when the thousand years of Christ's reign is ended, Satan shall be loosed for a little season. That little season shall come to an end when the Lord appears, casting Satan into the pit, sitting upon the great white throne, and assembling the world to the final judgment. The coming of the Lord draweth nigh, but the final judgment day is something more than a thousand years in the future.

Let us not forget that the rapture is to occur before the visible coming of the Lord. The bride is to be caught away in the air, is to be taken up to be with Jesus. Like the eight persons in the ark were brought into a place of safety while the flood destroyed the wicked world, so the saints of the Lord, the Bride of Christ, sometime, we know not when, are to be caught away out of the earth's turmoil and strife, and to be kept in peace and safety during the great tribulation. They are to come back with Jesus when He appears visibly to set up His kingdom.

Just as John the Baptist ran before our Lord at His first coming to prepare the way for the Master, so the great modern revival and missionary movement is a mighty John the Baptist, running before the second coming of our Lord to prepare for Him a bride. Let us be sure that we are washed, sanctified, tried and made white, and have on the wedding garment of righteousness when our Lord shall come and catch away His bride.

Writings of H.C.Morrison,D.D.

WORLD TOUR OF EVANGELISM.

An interesting and helpful missionary book written on his evangelistic tour of the world. 32 full-page illustrations. Neatly bound in cloth. $1.00.

LIFE SKETCHES AND SERMONS.

Story of the early life, conversion and sanctification of Bro. Morrison. Also a number of sermons. It has been greatly used in bringing people into the experience. Price, 50 cents.

THE TWO LAWYERS.

The truth put in story form, intensely interesting. At the same time the teaching of Holiness is brought out in a very forceful way. Buy it, enjoy it yourself and pass it along. Cloth binding, 50 cents. Paper 25 cents.

THE SECOND COMING OF CHRIST.

Rev. Hilary S. Westbrook says: "The best book I have ever read on the great subject of Christ coming back to earth again. It is written in superb style and each chapter is flowing with the milk of full salvation." Cloth, 50 cents.

BAPTISM WITH THE HOLY GHOST.

This is a very clear and concise statement of the subject and many persons have used quantities of them to good advantage. Price, 10 cents.

THE PEARL OF GREATEST PRICE.

A sermon on the 13th chapter of First Corinthians. Price, 10 cents.

THE CONFESSIONS OF A BACKSLIDER.

It is good reading, very interesting, and furnishes food for thought just as it is instructive and affords some good moral lessons. The booklet is fine for placing in the hands of young men just starting out in life, though it is not inappropriate for teachers in colleges and for parents as well. Price, 25 cents.

ROMANISM AND RUIN.

We are sending forth this book with an earnest desire to contribute something to the awakening of the American people to a proper appreciation of the dangers that now threaten our institutions and liberties.

THOUGHTS FOR THE THOUGHTFUL.

Rev. John Paul says: "It peals out like the notes of a deep-toned organ, each distinct. Sin is punctured, vanity is assailed; religious abuses are arraigned; the pearl of great price is held up to the reader and its aspects are shown in pungent paragraphs spaced off to themselves and making complete thoughts.. You can start on any page, you can stop on any page, and yet the book possesses unity." Price, 25 cents.

PROPHECIES FULFILLED AND FULFILLING.

The writing of this book was the product of much time and study, and in order that the public generally might have the benefit of his painstaking research, the author has put the lectures in book form, hoping thereby, to awaken the people to the fact that the present generation is living in the most marvelous time in the world's history. The author's arguments are unanswerable, and the prophecies cited are corroborated by the rapidly changing events in present-day movements. Price, 50 cents.

COMMENCEMENT SERMONS.

Some of Bro. Morrison's best sermons delivered at Asbury College, beautifully printed and bound in half leather, stamped in gold, gilt top. Price, 50 cents.

PENTECOSTAL PUBLISHING CO., Louisville, Ky.

www.ingramcontent.com/pod-product-compliance
Lightning Source LLC
Chambersburg PA
CBHW020508030426
42337CB00011B/281